# Who's Counting?

Shirley McClure

ᗅ

Acknowledgements:

Thanks are due to the editors of the following publications in which these poems first appeared:

*Poetry Life*, *The SHOp*, *The Stinging Fly*, *Bray Arts Club Journal*, *Galway Now*, *The Works*, *Revival*, *Boyne Berries*, *The Space Inside*, *Tributaries*, *Cyphers*, *Gates of Ivory and Horn* (Airfield Writers' anthology), *Shape Sifting* (Cinnamon Press Anthology), *Stand Magazine*.

Shirley McClure was born in Waterford and lives in Bray, Co. Wicklow. She took part in Poetry Ireland's Introductions Series in 2009 and was runner-up in the 2009 Patrick Kavanagh Award.

# Contents

MONTHS BEFORE SHE MET HIM

THE SMEARS OF THE WORLD

BREAD & BUTTER

*for* Philip

MONTHS BEFORE SHE MET HIM

# I

## Yoga Class

I skipped my yoga class
because the man was due
to fix the curtain rail.

Upstairs, he poised in heavy boots
on the edge of my bed,
but not before prudently
peeling back the elegant blue
Brown Thomas duvet.

Beneath him I stood
at optimal angle to flaunt
my cleavage, to hand him screws.

Smoothly he inserted the rawl plug,
then with slightly quicker breath
he drove it deep
into my freshly-painted, trembling
Orchid White walls.

Threading the hoops unto the pole
we lifted it together,
our fingers touching
as he tenderly
completed the work.

Later we did yoga together
dreamt up new asanas
and held them, and each other
until light began slinking through
my brand new curtains.

## Ring Road

I had a date last night.

He was polite,
told me *all* about
the new Ring Road
which hasn't yet been built-
and his own new house,
which he's building, floor
by door
by floor.

But how could I concentrate
on the Lisbon Treaty, or the cost
of cement,
when the whole wide story of *your* heart
lies almost unknown to me?

If it had been *you*, sipping latte,
telling the place names of your life,
I'd have hinged my eyes on the interval between
the cotton of your clothes
and your warm skin
and listened forever.

If only I could rest in that space
I suspect
that even the round ribbon
of ring roads waiting to be built
could cunningly
fill me
with wonder...

## Txt Sex

Text messaging,
the first hot Sunday in May–
he: I hope you're doing something
wild. I'm
busy with lambing.
She: Sun-bathing
out the back,
does that count as wild?
He: That depends
on how naked you are...

She pictures him delivering,
arm-deep
in placenta,
imagining her nakeder, fuller,
redder than she really is, outside
on a blue rug holding
a silver mobile phone.

She turns over, pale still,
unhooks her bra;
they joke about his sad life
chatting to sheep
phone dating,
dreaming of nakedness
in Edenbrook Heights.

If she were less prudent,
she'd ask him over now,
shower him, sponge each finger carefully,
massage his neck and armpits
with apricot soap;
but it's not like that with them,
his wedding band has left a mark
that no lamb's blood can cover.
She dresses, texts goodbye
and phones
the take-away.

# The Deer

Months before she met him
she was falling:
she'd seen his picture
in black and white,
Googled his life,
and heard
*something* of his reputation.

Months before she met him,
she knew,
she would drive headlong
to the earth's rim
just to see him live,
risking life and skin.

He was exactly as described:
a perfect, deep-throated
stag,
encircled
by dark-eyed, feisty does.

She knew,
as he unwrapped her heart,
that he was used to getting presents
like this;
even her breasts
stayed soft as he opened her,
confusing his hooves
with a skylark's wing.

Still later, as she combed his hair
with gratitude
-even though she'd always known-
it took everything she had
not to cry out
at the dark hair now covering her own arms
and her doe eyes reflected in his.

Months before she met him
she was falling.

## The Prison Officer

After a spate
of bankers
called Frank,
and I.T. heads
(mostly Evan or Ivan or Keith),
it felt like progress
to meet P.J., a P.O.
from Westmeath.

P.J. had a soft face,
well-meaning,
and a soft hidden apron of flesh
beneath his navy fleece.
He had friendly hands,
and a deep rich melting chocolate voice–
she saved his messages
to play back over and over.

He told her about work,
the inmates, their rights:
to see a doctor every day;
to go to mass on Holy Days.
*I think they have too many Holy Days*
*they should get rid of some of them*
*(by the way I like your hair–*
*do you dye it?)*

After a spate
of bankers
called Frank–
who as good as asked her
how much she earned–
it was different, anyway,
to hear about prison:
the rec yard, the fights,
the being liked,
not being called a screw–
what could be rarer, she thought,
than to live half your life Inside

and to like it.

## Over to You

I haven't felt like making any sweeping statements
since I met you.

You haven't bowled me over,
knocked me over with a feather;
I'm neither overjoyed
nor overawed.

But overall,
I haven't overlooked
your overarching possibilities.

Let's say our lives have
overlapped, and not to overstate it:
*I've overheard your thoughts–*
discreetly overheating.

So why don't we get overdressed,
I'll overcook you dinner,
you'll oversimplify your oversized
life story.

You'll overreach out for my hand,
I'll overcast all caution to the wind,

the wind will coil around our voices,
overcome us, overcome us.

## II

### Skin Problem

Once some guy has climbed on you,
grown on you, helped himself
to more of you,
nestled so nearly
under your skin
and then
abruptly
left

don't let it be said
you're an easily led,
easily lost,
misled, mislaid, mis-
ogynist-magnet

only
what do you do with
the bit of him that's left
under your thin,
middle-aged skin?

## Single Mind

I want to know
how you do it.
Have you learnt to erase me
from your single mind
or does some part of it, a lip
or a sigh, persist.

I want to know
how your body forgets me.
If that curious circle
of shade around your navel
has no memory, then surely
the hundred nerve endings
of your middle finger
must hanker for my skin.

And if you won't tell me,
and if I can't touch you,
I will pursue the dull eraser
as you pursued me,
I will befriend the empty mind,
as my body is emptied,
I will espouse the soul's stillness

beyond you,
beyond me,
beyond wanting.

## Dear Life

Sometimes it's as though
we hold on for dear life.
Squeeze, cling, draw each other near,
the tighter the safer,
the warmer you enfold me
the harder it is to concede
that this holding on stands
between you and your dear god
and me and my dear life.

## Hello Tina

He went to Dive School
for a week
on Inisturk.

Came back buoyed up
on oxygen, showed me
his Valsalva manoeuvre,
showed, like a toddler
mastering his letters,
his Underwater Plastic
Writing Slate,
on which stated
-dry as innocence-
"HELLO TINA".

In the photos he wore
mask tank fins
eyes frog-like,
in the photos Tina
in neoprene wetsuit
looked unnecessarily slim.

"We're all going
to the Red Sea
at Easter, Tina
and her mate
have set it up."

I decided there and then
to get serious, give me
a few weeks and I'd be
crazy about caverns,
a connoisseur
of Dead Man's Fingers,
an authority
on caves wrecks reeks.

Sink or snorkel
I would shimmy
with the darkness,
pioneer lost cities,
make friends
with bladderwrack
and giant clams
have the Great Whites eating
out of my hand.

# III

## The Spell

Instantly, you will know.
You will turn
from the book you will be reading
or the wood you will be turning
or the friend of a kind friend
who'll later introduce us.

There will be no crisis
of conversion,
since by then you will be dwelling
under clean slates, waiting
for the moment when
the collie at your heel
barks twice, makes eyes
at the collie at mine.

And in this version
of your certain future,
I will turn to you,
admire your dog's fine coat
and you will know, instantly.

## *Write Down Your Dreams*, He Said

I dreamt about your kitchen,
the firm leather skin
of the year's first pumpkin
yielding under stainless steel.

I dreamt about your fingers at my sacrum,
fastening the strings of your Italian apron;
your lunar-grey eyes intent
on onions darkening in oil.

And I dreamt about my own
ice-cold-from-scraping-the-potatoes fingers,
tracing the bold muscles of your neck
for the very first time;

the vibration of your softening breath,
a taste of berries. All this,
and the euphoria of stillness,
I dreamt about, till finally sleep came.

## Ambivalence

Your nearly-No
is so, so far
from my almost-Yes

that if I didn't
sort of
know you

I'd practically throw
my hat
at happiness.

## Who's Counting?

You wore contact lenses
for the first three dates
French Connection shirts
your warm cheeks shaved.

You brought yellow daisies
on every second date
refilled my wine glass
after every second taste.

You played me Gershwin
braised me tofu
praised my textures
oiled my shoulders
wormed my compost
turned my corners

said you loved me
on the sixty-second date.

## New Boyfriend's Party

I am not a diva,
my voice will not break windows
nor my deep dress dazzle your eyes.
I do not know the moves,
the notes, the nuances
that hurl a room
into a thirsty silence.

And when the people come,
instead of easing a path
between the unknown species,
I will hover too long
amongst the well-tilled borders
of my friends, or

finding foreign courage
will, clasping my machete,
slice needlessly
into the clinking air.

Until suddenly
I've left it too late
and they're all standing up
and making nodding noises

*and we must meet soon*
*you must come to dinner*
*let's meet soon and* **chat**
*and lovely to meet you*

and my sleep is filled
with the wise and witty things
I didn't say.

Instead
I am awake before you
counting bottles
dousing surfaces
raking cheesecake into sticky bins
raising damp napkins
from the crevices of seats

cooling my head
with the unworldliness of tea.

## Good Friday Planting

I release my suitcase,
catch you shirtless, shaving,
clay and purpose
in your finger-nails,
a gold-ribboned egg
on the kitchen table.

First earlies,
your welcome home gift to me.
I'm away a week
and you're talking about
Red Dukes of York,
Charlottes, Edzell Blues,
the anticipated thrill
of lifting your first haulm.

I lift your fingers to my mouth,
taste phosphorus, potassium,
a trace of dibbled tubers;
savour the salty
afternoon drills of your chest.

Later, later we will feast
on Sharpe's Early Express.

## Made to Measure

Does it make sense, any more,
to set it out in neatly raised beds?
To measure love with reference
to the earth's diameter,
the leagues between the poles,
the space between my sternum
and my spine? Does the old stuff
about the planets still apply?
Didn't Shakespeare cover all that?

Should we not talk of love
in terms of kilojoules?
Combine our circuit boards,
get close in mega-pixels?
In the new century
do we not calculate intensity
in coloured dots?
Make love in dpi?

But still there is the precious gap
between this afternoon and now,
the dip and dive of swallows
on a green road hemmed by fuschia.
Your camera describes foxgloves,
flag iris, teasel and me;
and between Bull's Head
and Knocknadobar
there is yet space for us
that can't be counted.

# Dream Wedding

We had chilli ramen last night,
a satay sauce, a burgundy
too sturdy for my stomach.

Aer Lingus had a sale till midnight
so we put our money down
-red kisses at the keyboard-
New England honeymoon.

I dreamt about a woman
at our wedding; yellow noodles
dangled from her mouth,
you smiled at her
and flicked them away
with your tongue.

In the dream I roared at you,
demanded nothing less
than all my money back.

This morning when I told you,
smooth-shaven, hot press fresh,
you just kissed me softly and said–
*no noodles at our wedding.*

# THE SMEARS OF THE WORLD

# Gardener
### *for my father*

Tonight my house is bursting with sympathetic
flowers:
crinkled white carnations
upright in every vase;
baby's breath exhaling from the glasses;
lilies filling every jug.

I want to repaint all the walls magenta,
the doors cerulean blue,
buy daffodils to launch spring early,
replace every gerbera and freesia,
every sober eskimo rose.

At least you got to see the snowdrops
I carried to your bedside
in wicker baskets cushioned with moss
(Protestant flowers, my cousin said).

But all the colours that you planted
wait still, biding their time
in company with you
under winter's desolate garden.

## Metastasis

In his last weeks
he sends a dozen letters,
makes recompense,
receives his friends,
talks, tires, takes tablets,
holds each person near.

The house itself
has folded in its corners,
walls warm and soften
to accommodate his waning,
medicine gets stronger,
death is just behind him
and he starts to slip,
spits blood,
has the bishop pray
above his head.

In his last days
he is stoned on morphine,
grins wide-eyed at the high of it;
then there is only sleep.
Time stretched with concern
for his poor body,
turning him,
moistening his tongue,
oiling his dried lips,
scenting the room
with lavender and rosemary.

In his last moments
there is just my father;
his gasps,
each vying
not to be the last one;
and we three women,
sharing his hands
and brow between us,
talking him through,
sending him on,
in spite of us.

# Remembrance

On Christmas Eve morning
my mother crafts three wreaths
for the recent dead.

At the last one, my father's,
she sinks holly and chrysanthemums
in a ring of quicksand.

We bear them like frankincense
silent down Maudlin Street, oasis
suckling our finger-tips;

I unlock the church gate
lean over
freshly cut stone.

From over the road, outside Langton's
-even as we whisper our greetings-
flies a loaded taunt:
"She's a fine arse-for a Protestant!"

# Washing Dishes for my Mother

Uncovered,
the tight-bound, spring-coloured heart
of a butterhead lettuce,

one of the last things on earth
I can offer you.

I clatter dishes,
you wait in the half-dark
for a supper that will not sustain you.

Later, hands drop
into grateful water,
wishing these dishes would continue forever.

If this
were all that was left to me,
it would contain me:

my hands
on your plate and cup
in a moss-green basin

purposeful,
wiping away
the smears of the world.

## Before Cancer

I don't want to think of you
hopeless on a metal bed,
choice ebbing from your limbs.

I want to remember you industrious,
baking meringues first thing
on a Saturday morning.

I don't want to think of you immobile,
terrified of forfeiting everything.

I want to remember you electric,
wagging a finger, censorious,
"Oh Shir, you're such a mimic!"

I need to conjure you sure-footed,
threading a path between sycamores,
harvesting loganberries,
saving dried quinces on a Spanish plate.

I need to think of you before metastasis,
Tamoxifen and Dexamethasome
became your daily bread.

Instead I am suspended
in a February morning,

bringing you a cupful of snow
from the hospital car park,
holding your strong left hand,

ice fading
in our fingers.

## Calling To Me Through The Woods

I have gone out searching for you
in amongst the thick-knit spruces
at the place where the fire-break peters
in the hours when birds sleep
and long-boned alsatians crouch
alongside last night's bonfire.

I have carried no torch
for fear of waking the living
just bluebells
and foxgloves and rosemary
and the torn part of me that aches
for your stout-hearted stillness.

But you are in hiding
fastened with the moss, maybe,
to the river wall,
upstanding with the heron
or endurance swimming
with the wisest salmon
back bravely to the dark Atlantic salt.

## Sustainable Dying

Wrap me in sack-cloth
and bury me under
our Guaranteed Irish
permaculture plot.

Let no formaldehyde
sully my creases
but bathe me in organic
Fair Trade frankincense.

I'll forgo cremation–
my previous first option–
since it's such a frittering
of priceless fuel.

Plant me under blackberries
and when your lips grow dark
be in no doubt–
I gave you sweetness.

## Exact Science

On Christmas Eve
he draws it all out
on the page.

The senior surgeon,
red-eyed from poring over
wayward stars,
makes no bones about
calling a sign a sign.

Prince of the modern Magi,
he lays out his thesis,
antithesis, then erases both:

*Of course
it's your own decision.*

## Mastectomy

You get given
certain things in twos–

      love-birds, book-ends,
      matching china tea mugs–

and even though
on any given morning

      it is all you even think of
      to hook one fine china

top designer
duck-blue tea-mug

      from your dry beech
      draining rack

to boil and pour and stir
and watch Darjeeling towers spiral;

      there are still the days
      when there is company for breakfast,

and on these fine mornings
let me tell you

      it is good to know
      that there are two

extra special, same but different
unchipped breakfast blue mugs

       made to grace
your table.

## Menopause

She's been loitering,
squeezing by
in soft-tailored XL suits,
her hints at wisdom,
promises of power
disguising her shape.

I meet her in the shower,
free-falling breasts
lounge across the creases
of her belly. She teases me,
cries *nonsense, clinging*
*to the cramping calendar of youth*
*when freedom is at hand.*

And now some magic pill's
going to catapult me
forward in years, high-speed me
pouting and railing
to the palace of the crone;
sweat me, dry me, whisper me
the secrets, make me *mature*
before my time.

# Reconstructed

At her kitchen table
in the stark morning
of New Year's day,
a woman I've just met
spreads marmalade
on toasted soda bread,
recounts the ins and outs
of losing both her breasts.

Before I know it
in her keenness
to prepare me
as no doctor could,
she is pushing aside
cups and crumbs,
pulling wool and cotton
up over her ribs,
straining to unhook
her hospital-white bra.

Faced with the tender
drumlins of her chest,
each raked with
a flat red seam,
I am swept away
that it is she
who is consoling me,
her wise heart
which has remained
inviolate.

## The Fitting

With dressmakers' measure
the stylish surgeon
sizes up my breast.

Her buffed and polished fingers
range and dart from rib to nipple
she whispers numbers,
fourteen, seven, seven.

Practised hands
flick through a catalogue
select a replica,
to get me even.

We talk wedding plans
the dress, the date,
she counsels on décolletage

Next month, she will cut
and stretch and boost and stitch,
fit for my wedding day
make me a match.

## Waiting List

The new breast
is always fridge-cool.

Hot-palm its pleats
it is teen-pert,
bra-perfect,
soap-stone round.

Tracked across
the almost-centre
puffy-concertinaed
where they sewed it up,
a fist's width
below the oxter.

Still nippleless,
I am a polished moonstone
lady-in-waiting.

BREAD & BUTTER

## Cinnamon

A trendy, chi chi,
old-style, new-style cafe,
Queen's Park, London

savouring my two best friends
like morning buns
like melted yellow butter
drizzled over hungry tongues

enabled by the secrets of Lavazza,
smooth sticks of Madagascar,

to tell everything we know
whisper everything we feel
-no spice spared.

## Bus Fellows (Spain 1990)

He speaks without teeth–
he must be sixty–
in a language I don't quite remember,
something about my throat
and a lorry-load of goats
awaiting him in Ronda

Clamped between him
and the coach window
his elbow niggles my side
and sticky hands
fiddle with his fly.

He woos without teeth
in the universal language of intrusion.
I spit back–definitely–NO!
and conjure up,
should there be any room for doubt,
a lorry-load of husbands
awaiting me in Ronda.

# Eurogreen

Hand-sewn hemp intimates
from Kathmandu,

sasawashi suits are made-to-measure,

mud baths in Bad Kissingen
skilleted tofu,

she's eco-chic, she's über-clean
she's green forever.

Frocks dyed with fraughans
from Mullaghcleevaun,

water is lab-tested as a rule,

exfoliates with sea-salt
has her eye-brows drawn,

she's eco-chic, she's über-clean
she's no green fool.

Sponsored trees in São Luís
Minke whales in Mull,

offset a mini-break in Nîmes,

her euros may be green, darling,
but life is never dull,

she's eco-chic, she's über-clean
forever green.

## Travelling Companions Wanted

Bearded, serene
ornithologist, Assisi,
seeks fellow travellers
(preferably male)
for wildlife safari.
First Aid a bonus.
May have problems
with bleeding.

Contact: Francesco

Fun-loving,
original fruitarian, female,
seeks man for city breaks,
naturism, anywhere
but gardens.
Snake phobia.

Contact: Eve

German woman, blonde,
long hair to die for,
seeks well-connected guy
for abseiling, fun times,
will make it worth your while,
will teach you
the secret of stillness
if you can just get me
out of here.

Contact: Rapunzel

Likely lad, U.K.,
seeks mates, up
for a bit of mullarkey,
must have martial arts
and sprint fast
at high altitudes.
Best blokes get nest-eggs
like what you've never seen.

Contact: Jack

## Not Coffee

I want my coffee to be
brisk and rich and muscular.

I want my coffee
to nuzzle me awake,
a tongue of brightness
filtered through my bedroom window.

I want my coffee sonorous,
to call my name from cafe terraces,
mosaic tables shaded from the midday sun.

I want my coffee ceremonial,
a daily Event.

I am trying to adjust to Dandelion,
to its flat, thin sweetness,

loath to admit it's the bitterness I miss.

## For Rachael

You have evolved
from scattiest girl
to junior baker.

You measure flour and sugar,
know with the confident alchemy of cooks,
to omit the baking powder.

You crack an egg and giggle
at the one long line
formed in its side.

*I only use eggs,*
you tell me,
*from Woodville Farm.*

At almost twelve
you have become your mother
thirty-two years ago

piling moist ginger snaps,
banana bread and carrot cake
into the sweet-toothed mouth of the Aga.

Then as now
I looked on, made myself useless
to the best of my ability.

Until recently
it looked like you took after me,
haphazard middle child–

I must not begrudge you
a clatter of your mother's talents;
bake on, sweet niece,

keep a little for me.

## Half-way Home

It was a live-in situation
at the Liverpool hostel
for homeless men.
For full board
and twenty quid a month
I mopped floors, played pool,
changed urine-soaked sheets,
wheeled Mikey to the pub
on a Wednesday, after the pension.

He asked me awkward questions
about marriage, sobbed when I said
it wasn't in my plans, "But
did your mother not explain?"
Once or twice he threw me
a hundred pounds,
which had been mouldering
under his mattress.

The cook had cystitis,
she said I was the fattest vegetarian
she'd ever seen. Tommy
was on hormone treatment
for a female to male sex change,
and Billy held his yellow-grey head
as he paced, "Rainhill,
Rainhill is my home,
Rainhill, Rainhill, Rainhill
is my home."

On Christmas day there was beer
and cigarettes and crackers,
I sneaked my boyfriend in
and we lay listening
in my attic room:
*Oh come all ye faithful,*
*Joyful and triumphant,*
*Rainhill, Rainhill,*
*Rainhill is my home.*

*Rainhill: the psychiatric hospital in Liverpool*